Young Playwrights' Theater Presents

# Voices from the Valley:
## Plays by the Fourth Graders of Garcia Elementary School

A collection of 33 outstanding plays from the 2013-14 fourth graders of Graciela Garcia Elementary School

Young Playwrights' Theater

Young Playwrights' Theater (YPT) is the only professional theater in Washington, DC dedicated entirely to arts education. By teaching students to express themselves through the art of playwriting, YPT develops students' language skills, and empowers them with the creativity, confidence and critical thinking skills they need to succeed in school and beyond. YPT honors its students by involving them in a high-quality artistic process where they feel simultaneously respected and challenged and by engaging professional theater artists in producing student plays for the community.

# Introduction

by YPT Teaching Artist Catherine DiSanza

When I began working with Young Playwrights' Theater (YPT) in Washington, DC, I immediately found that the organization's mission and approach to education were unique. YPT inspires young people to realize the power of their own voices, developing students' language skills through the art of playwriting and empowering them with the creativity, confidence and critical thinking skills they need to succeed in school and beyond. By integrating playwriting into the English Language Arts curriculum, YPT teaches students to analyze literature and express themselves clearly through speaking and writing.

Most significantly, YPT values students as artists who have important stories to share and who can make valuable contributions to their communities. When YPT brings actors into the classroom to perform students' work or produces student-written theater in the community, young people see the significance of their ideas and their ability to move an audience. In my time in DC, I saw that firsthand. Many of my students started the program saying that they didn't like or "weren't good at" writing, and, by the end, discovered they do indeed have a talent for and enjoy writing. Through YPT, I saw DC's young people build confidence as they overcame the challenging parts of writing and surprised themselves with their achievements. I saw them learn to express and advocate for themselves.

I knew that YPT's work would be valuable to students not just in DC but around the country. When my husband and I moved to McAllen in 2013, I couldn't wait to share the joy of playwriting with young people right here in the Valley. Students in this region have such unique stories to tell: stories of being part of two cultures and speaking two languages, stories of pride in their families and community. It is important for their voices to be heard, and I felt strongly that playwriting would be a great way for them to share their experiences.

When I met Principal Yolanda Castillo, I knew that Garcia Elementary in Pharr would be the perfect partner school for the pilot of YPT's ***In-School Playwriting Program*** in Texas. Principal Castillo and the teachers employ an innovative, bilingual International Baccalaureate curriculum. Integrating playwriting into the Language Arts curriculum fit in well with the school's unique pedagogical approach. The program would not have been possible without the incredible support of the teachers and administrators who were involved throughout the process and provided guidance and encouragement to the student playwrights. They believed in the students and in the power of arts education.

The students at Garcia put their hearts into the writing process. Some were immediately confident about their ability to write a play, and others were unsure. However, each student persevered through the challenging parts of the writing process and every student wrote an original play, a task not many adults have completed. Most students wrote in their second language, and eagerly put in the additional time and effort to do so.

The incredible imaginations and persistent hard work of the fourth graders brought forth this exciting selection of plays. In this book, magic abounds, stuffed animals come to life and zombies attack. Students express their values in plays such as *Revenge of the Wolves* and explore issues common to us all, such as rivalry within families and the struggle to make good friends. I am very proud of these students and happy to be able to share their work.

# Dedication

by Graciela Garcia Elementary School Principal Yolanda Castillo

I dedicate this edition of short student plays to all our parents and staff who have nurtured and encouraged our students to become interactive players in the process of writing these plays.

Indeed, the entire staff is profoundly indebted to Catherine DiSanza and Young Playwrights' Theater, who taught, inspired and helped students organize their thoughts and ideas.

Graciela Garcia Elementary is a Pre-Kindergarten through 5th grade campus located three miles from the Mexican border in the south side of Pharr, Texas. The school has been in operation since 2001. The enrollment is 774 students, 99% of which are Hispanics, and 100% of the students participate in free or reduced National Lunch Program. In addition 81% are classified as Limited English Proficient (ELL). Furthermore, 95% of these students are labeled "at risk" of not graduating from high school.

In spite of these statistics, Graciela Garcia continues to beat the odds. Garcia Elementary received the Texas Education Agency's designation as a 2013-2014 High Performance School, becoming the only elementary school in the Pharr-San Juan-Alamo Independent School District to receive this recognition and also acquired six stars. Garcia Elementary is the only Dual Language and International Baccalaureate School in the district.

Many of these short plays come from the children's family and cultural experiences. These plays will help you recognize your child's uniqueness and abilities.

May you enjoy these sweet, funny, short plays written by our very own Graciela Garcia fourth grade students.


With pride,

Yolanda Castillo
Principal

# Table of Contents

# Dog and Animal Control

by Derek Irvegas

Characters:
ANIMAL CONTROL
DOG

*SCENE 1:*

ANIMAL CONTROL: *(Angry voice)* Get over here you mutt!

DOG: Never!

ANIMAL CONTROL: I'm so tired of trying to catch this dog, it is so hard! It's useless. *(Sad voice)* I'm never going to catch him.

DOG: He's never going to find me here.

ANIMAL CONTROL: Hey get over here! I should follow him.

DOG: I just want to be free!!

ANIMAL CONTROL: I will catch you if it takes forever!

DOG: *(Whining voice)* He's never going to leave me alone.

ANIMAL CONTROL: Look, I just want to adopt you so you can be free.

DOG: Really?

ANIMAL CONTROL: NO!!!!!! I just want to catch you.

DOG: Too bad. *(Running away)* Try to catch me.

ANIMAL CONTROL: *(Angry voice)* Ahhhhh! *(Chases after him.)* I'm coming! *(Trips and falls.)* Ouch.

DOG: Haha!!!! You can't catch me, I'm too fast you are too slow.

ANIMAL CONTROL: I'm faster than you, you will see. *(Running faster)*

DOG: *(Trapped)* No!

ANIMAL CONTROL: Haha!!!!!!!!!!!!!!!!

DOG: Look, if you don't catch me I'll give you money.

ANIMAL CONTROL: You don't even have money.

DOG: *(Confused voice)* How did you know?

ANIMAL CONTROL: I didn't know until now.

DOG: Darn it!!!

ANIMAL CONTROL: You can't trick me.

DOG: I'll give you a car!!!

ANIMAL CONTROL: Nice try.

DOG: How about a house?

ANIMAL CONTROL: I already have a house.

DOG: So you don't want anything?

ANIMAL CONTROL: Yes I do, I want to catch you.

DOG: Why?

ANIMAL CONTROL: So you can go somewhere safe and where there's food.

DOG: Really?!

ANIMAL CONTROL: Yes.

DOG: Okay, I'll go with you.

*SCENE 2:* *In a dog park by the lake.*

DOG: Wow, I love it here, thanks Animal Control. I see white juicy bones, food and water on the ground. I smell flowers. I taste dog food. I hear dogs barking. I feel water splashing. I think it is the best world ever.

*End of Play*

# Toto and the Rainforest

by Grace Santana

Characters:
TOTO
GRACE
MR. SANTANA
MRS. SANTANA
EMILY
FRANKIE
SAMMY
GOD 1
GOD 2
GOD 3

_SCENE 1:_ _In the kitchen._

_(TOTO walks into the kitchen with his PJs on, there he sees GRACE and her family.)_

TOTO: I just finished reading a book about the rainforest, it was very interesting. _(He grabs a plate of chocolate chip cookies and a glass of milk.)_

GRACE: Toto, where are you going?

TOTO: I'm going to my room to read another book. _(He takes the cookies and the glass of milk to his room.)_

EMILY: Why do you always need to look after him? _(EMILY takes a bite from her pancake.)_

MR. SANTANA: After all, he won't be your little stuffed dog forever.

_SCENE 2:_ _In TOTO's room._

_(TOTO is in his room reading another book and eating his chocolate chip cookies and drinking his glass of milk.)_

TOTO: Wow! I didn't know you could go to the rainforest.

_(TOTO goes to GRACE's room. There GRACE is painting her nails and listening to loud music.)_

TOTO: Mom, I want to go to a rainforest.

GRACE: WHAT!!!!!

TOTO: TURN YOUR MUSIC OFF MOM!!!!

_(GRACE turns off her music and stops painting her nails.)_

TOTO: I want to go to a rainforest.

GRACE: Toto, I'm sorry but you can't go.

TOTO: What? _(Starts crying.)_ FINE! Why did you ever choose me to be your son.

GRACE: Toto, I chose you because you were different than all the other stuffed animals. *(Starts crying too.)*

TOTO: Whatever. I'll be in my room. "Sniff." *(Stops crying and goes to his room.)*

MR. AND MRS. SANTANA: What is all the commotion!

EMILY AND FRANKIE: Hey quiet! We are watching a marathon about a monkey showing his butt every time he eats!

SAMMY: Eeeh, I don't care.

MRS. SANTANA: Why was Toto crying?

GRACE: I told him he can't go to the rainforest. *(Stops crying.)*

SAMMY: I take it back, I do care— he's my favorite stuffed animal.

MRS. SANTANA: You are right.

*SCENE 3:* In TOTO's room.

*(TOTO is in his room sleeping. After a few hours he wakes up and sees his THREE GODS.)*

GOD 1: I think he's awake.

GOD 2: Of course he's awake, you dork.

GOD 3: Guys, be serious.

TOTO: Who are you? *(Scratches his head.)*

GODS: *(Together)* We are your three gods.

GOD 3: We will grant you one wish.

TOTO: Okay, I wish I could go to the rainforest.

GOD 2: As you wish.

*(The THREE GODS take TOTO to the rainforest. GRACE walks into TOTO's room.)*

GRACE: Toto, I'm sorry, okay. Toto where are you?

*(Back to the rainforest.)*

TOTO: I want to go back to my home.

GOD 1: As you wish.

*(TOTO appears back in his room, there he sees GRACE.)*

GRACE: Toto I'm sorry.

TOTO: I am sorry too, I'm such a jerk.

GRACE: To show you that I am sorry we will go to the rainforest. But you have to write an essay for me.

TOTO: Yes! Okay. But how?

GRACE: My dad worked extra shifts. Plus we got to get packing.

TOTO: Okay.

GRACE'S FAMILY: We got to get moving.

*(GRACE, TOTO and her FAMILY hug each other.)*

*End of Play*

# My Brother and My Doll

by Michelle Sanchez

Characters:
SYLVIA, MICHELLE's doll
DANIEL, MICHELLE's brother
MICHELLE

*SCENE 1:* DANIEL's room.

*(SYLVIA enters.)*

SYLVIA: I see my friend's brother coming. I smell his stinky shoes. I taste the lollipop he ate last night. I hear his footsteps. I feel my heart beating faster each time. I think he is going to destroy me. *(Beat)* Hi Daniel. *(She looks scared.)* You are scaring me so you need to stop it.

DANIEL: I'm thinking of destroying you.

SYLVIA: Me? Why?

DANIEL: Once my sister destroyed all my cars and flushed them down the toilet.

SYLVIA: *(Crying)* Then that's why you want to destroy me.

DANIEL: *(Laughing)* Don't cry or I will throw you on the floor.

*SCENE 2:* Outside in the backyard.

DANIEL: Hello Sylvia, are you ready to run for your life like in the Hunger Games?

SYLVIA: What do you mean?

DANIEL: Yes in the Hunger Games you had to run for your life.

SYLVIA: Oh really. I just want you to leave me alone.

DANIEL: If you want me to leave you alone you need to work for me and give me a massage every day.

SYLVIA: I'm going to get tired.

DANIEL: Then here comes the axe! This is going to hurt!

*Scene 3:* In MICHELLE's room.

*(MICHELLE enters.)*

MICHELLE: What are you doing with my doll and that axe?

DANIEL: I'm going to destroy your doll Sylvia!

MICHELLE: *(Screaming)* NOOOOOOOO! Give me back my doll or I will tell Mom.

DANIEL: Please no she is going to hit me!

MICHELLE: Okay. *(Waits for her doll.)*

DANIEL: Fine. *(Hands MICHELLE the doll.)*

MICHELLE: Thank you!!

DANIEL: I will get you later you dumb doll. Hahaha.

*End of Play*

# *Untitled*

by Daniel Zamora

Characters:
ALEX, Daniel's tablet
DANIEL
MOM
DRAGON
SOLDIERS
GUARD
MUMMY

*SCENE 1:* *At DANIEL's house.*

ALEX: I want a friend.

DANIEL: But there's only one left in China. Now I have to go to school.

*(Daytime.)*

DANIEL: Bye.

ALEX: Bye.

*(DANIEL shuts the door.)*

ALEX: I won't give up. *(Packs food in a backpack.)*

*(DANIEL comes back from school.)*

DANIEL: Alex, Alex, Alex, Mom where's Alex!

MOM: I saw him run out the door.

DANIEL: Oh no, he's going to China!

*SCENE 2:* *Near China.*

ALEX: So sleepy! OH look a cave.

*(ALEX feels breathing on his neck.)*

ALEX: Ahhh!!!!

DRAGON: Wait, I won't hurt you!

ALEX: You- you- you won't?

DRAGON: No, I just want a friend.

ALEX: You can be my friend if you tell me how much more I need to walk to get to China.

DRAGON: 40 miles.

ALEX: What!!

DRAGON: Get on my back, I'll fly to China.

*(Chinese people freak out.)*

SOLDIERS: Shoot the net gun!

DRAGON: Ah! We're going down. Pum!

ALEX: I forgot we need a map that's in Egypt.

DRAGON: It's my pleasure to get out of here.

*SCENE 3:* In Egypt.

DRAGON: *(At the cave)* I sense the map in this cave.

ALEX: Well let's go in.

MUMMY: Rah!!

DRAGON: Duck!

*(DRAGON breathes fire.)*

ALEX: Well that was easy.

*(Rocks start falling.)*

ALEX: Run!!

*(DRAGON picks up ALEX and they fly back to China.)*

*SCENE 4:* In China.

ALEX: Wait! We need to sneak past the guards.

DRAGON: Look, this sewer hole.

*(DRAGON digs dirt.)*

ALEX: Finally.

*(GUARD sees them.)*

SOLDIERS: Shoot the hose!

*(ALEX shuts down.)*

SOLDIERS: Shoot the sleeping dart!

*(DRAGON falls asleep.)*

*SCENE 4:* At DANIEL's house.

*(DANIEL is sent a note.)*

DANIEL: Sorry that we shot a hose at your tablet, we will fix it and bring it as good as new.

*(Two years pass.)*

DANIEL: Mom, they finally sent Alex!

ALEX: Sorry I left.

DANIEL: No, I'm sorry, now let's get you a friend.

*End of Play*

# Revenge of the Wolves

by Sarahi Farias

Characters:
CLAUDINA, a wolf
GUARD
WOLF HUNTER (KING), the king

*SCENE 1: CLAUDINA sniffs the air and smells fire. She tastes smoky air, she hears wolves howling in pain, she feels a sharp pain in her tail and she thinks humans are attacking!*

WOLF HUNTER (KING): I want you to get more fur.

GUARD: But, there are no wolves.

WOLF HUNTER (KING): I don't care, just go find more somewhere else or it's off with your head!

GUARD: *(Thinking)* Jeesh, he is such a jerk.

CLAUDINA: King, I will do anything you want.

WOLF HUNTER (KING): The only thing I want is your powerful fur!

CLAUDINA: King, please! Have mercy! I will give you all the fur you want.

WOLF HUNTER (KING): I know that you will run away and tell your pack to destroy me and my army. And if I win and you lose and die, I will get your fur and everyone will get under my spell and bow to me!

CLAUDINA: *(Crying)* Why do you want to get me!?

WOLF HUNTER (KING): *(Breathing heavily)* I want your fur to rule the world, because your fur is powerful.

CLAUDINA: Stop please! You evil jerk!

*(CLAUDINA howls because the KING scratches her with his knife.)*

CLAUDINA: You have gone too far, hunter!

WOLF HUNTER (KING): OH really? Well I am more powerful than you, Claudina! *(Pushes CLAUDINA into a wall.)*

*(CLAUDINA pushes him and throws an arrow at him and it hits his shoulder.)*

WOLF HUNTER (KING): Ugh. *(Breathing heavily)* I will get you one day, Claudina! *(The KING falls off the balcony and dies.)*

CLAUDINA: Victory is ours! Now guards please protect us, we need you.

GUARDS: Yes we will, and also thank you for killing the King. He was a really big jerk!

CLAUDINA: You're welcome. And if you need anything I am here for you.

*End of Play*

# Tiger Star

by Natasha de la Rosa

Characters:
TIGER STAR, a toy tiger
MR. J, an evil wizard
MONKEY, a toy monkey
SELLER PEOPLE, work in the toy store
CINDY, Mr. J's daughter
KELSY, Cindy's friend
NARRATOR

_SCENE 1:_ _In the toy store._

TIGER STAR: I see other stuffed animals. They don't mind being stuffed animals. I smell cotton. I taste fabric and cotton. I hear kids saying to their parents, "I want a stuffed animal." I feel the basket I am in. I think, "Where am I going to go?"

MR. J: How much does this stuffed animal cost?

SELLER PEOPLE: 39 dollars.

MR. J: _(Angrily)_ What!! 39 dollars for a stuffed animal?

SELLER PEOPLE: Yes sir.

TIGER STAR: _(Talking to MONKEY)_ Hey that's Mr. J, the meanest guy in the whole world. He is a wizard.

MONKEY: Are you sure?

TIGER STAR: Yes, I am sure.

MONKEY: Want to be a real Tiger? Go ask him.

TIGER STAR: Are you crazy!! He can turn you into a frog or statue!

MONKEY: Wow he is scary. It looks like he has a daughter.

TIGER STAR: His daughter is a wicked witch.

MR. J: Oh my gosh, I think he heard us talking to each other.

MONKEY: I think my mom is calling.

TIGER STAR: I didn't hear her.

MONKEY: I don't want to get in trouble bye!!

CINDY: Daddy, Daddy, I want a stuffed animal.

MR. J: Which one do you want?

15

CINDY: I want that kitty.

MR. J: How much does this cost?

SELLER PEOPLE: 29 dollars sir, and aren't you the meanest wizard in all the world?

MR. J: If you don't give me that for 5 dollars—

SELLER PEOPLE: What did you say?

MR. J: Give it to me for 5 dollars!

SELLER PEOPLE: What did you say?

MR. J: Give it to me for 5 dollars!

TIGER STAR: I am gonna make myself invisible so I can go and steal the potion from Mr. J.

MR. J: Well, I am going to my house. Cindy!

CINDY: Coming Daddy.

TIGER STAR: I am now going to Mr. J's house.

*SCENE 2:* At MR. J's house.

TIGER STAR: I am at Mr. J's house.

*(Sound effect: Pum! Pum!)*

MR. J: There is someone here.

CINDY: Are you sure, Daddy?

MR. J: Yes little one. Did you feel something, Cindy?

CINDY: No Daddy.

TIGER STAR: *(Whispering)* Monkey, open the door.

MONKEY: Is that you? Are you dead?

TIGER STAR: Oh you are so dumb, I am at the door.

MONKEY: Oh okay, I thought you were there.

TIGER STAR: He saw me. Oh that was so scary. He almost caught me.

MONKEY: Oh, now how am I going to copy your homework?

TIGER STAR: Is that what you are worried about?

MONKEY: No about you, and the homework.

TIGER STAR: Monkey!

MONKEY: Okay.

TIGER STAR: There is a better way. I need that potion.

NARRATOR: So she didn't get the potion and she did Plan B because Plan A didn't work. So she is going to make herself little.

MONKEY: I have a potion.

TIGER STAR: Why didn't you say?

MONKEY: You never asked.

TIGER STAR: What potion? Wait, Mr. J is here.

MR. J: That was weird last night. Kelsy's here to play.

CINDY: Okay Daddy.

KELSY: Hey girl how you doing?

CINDY: Good.

KELSY: Want to play?

CINDY: Yes, bye.

KELSY: Bye.

MR. J: Come Cindy.

CINDY: Coming Daddy. Byeee!

MR. J: *(Angrily)* Cindy!

CINDY: Okay.

KELSY: Bye.

MR. J: Kelsy want to live at our house?

CINDY: Say yes say yes!

KELSY: *(Excited and yelling)* OOOOOOOOOKAY.

CINDY: We are gonna have a lot of fun.

TIGER STAR: What do you need to do so the potion will work?

MONKEY: You drink the potion and it makes you little.

TIGER STAR: Well... *(Drinking the potion)* gun gun. Mmm, well I am going to Mr. J's house.

MR. J: Cindy get into the car.

17

CINDY: *(Sad and bored)* Okay.

NARRATOR: Well Mr. J went driving while Tiger Star went in a bicycle. Well Tiger Star got there and she almost got the potion.

TIGER STAR: *(Whispering)* La la la la la.

*(Chuc chuc goes the door.)*

MR. J: Cindy go to your room.

CINDY: Yes Dad.

TIGER STAR: *(Whispering)* Almost reach it, aaa!

MR. J: Let me check my potions. Mmmm...

TIGER STAR: Oh no, he is coming. I got to go!

MR. J: I think I heard something.

TIGER STAR: Oh no, I didn't get the transforming potion!

NARRATOR: So Tiger Star didn't get what she wanted and Mr. J got a little suspicious. So she went with a Plan C and she figured out why her plans didn't work.

TIGER STAR: I know the problem: every time I go to steal the potion from Mr. J he goes at the same time I go.

MONKEY: Well Mr. J is coming, get ready Tiger Star.

TIGER STAR: Well wish me good luck.

MONKEY: Yes, I wish you some good luck.

NARRATOR: So Tiger Star went to Mr. J's house and got the potion. After she got it, Mr. J came.

TIGER STAR: Yes! *(Whispering)* Yes yes yes! I got the potion! I got the potion!

MR. J: Cindy!

CINDY: I know, go to your room.

MR. J: No, want to help me?

CINDY: Yes!

MR. J: I called Kelsy's parents and asked them if she can come to play and they said yes.

CINDY: *(Yelling and excited)* Oh thank you! Oh thank you! I love you so much!

MR. J: She is coming.

TIGER STAR: Got it! I am going to the store with Monkey he will be so proud!

MONKEY: I am sure this time he got her.

TIGER STAR: Monkey, open the door!

MONKEY: Okay you got the potion, now you can turn yourself into a real tiger.

TIGER STAR: I wanted to ask you if you want be a real monkey.

MONKEY: Yes! Well what are we doing here? Let's go and drink that potion!

NARRATOR: And they drink the potion and they went to the zoo.

MONKEY: Bye Tiger Star! See you at breakfast.

TIGER STAR: You too.

NARRATOR: So Tiger Star got the transforming potion and turned Monkey and herself into real animals and lived happily ever after.

*End of Play*

# *Untitled*

by Teresa Garza

Characters:
BUBBLE
HEROBRIAN
VOICE, a voice in BUBBLE's head

*SCENE 1:* *In a park close to the benches.*

BUBBLE: I see kids, games, adults, grass, sun, my phone. I smell food from a picnic, perfume. I taste a sandwich that I took for lunch, juice, ice cream. I hear kids laughing, cats meowing, dogs barking. I feel someone bump into me, I feel like I'm flying! I think, wow! I am flying!! How did this happen? *(Excited voice)* No one will ever believe what happened to me a few days ago. I was in the park, this is what happened.

BUBBLE: *(Texting her friend)* OMG! My friend is going to love the dress that I will buy her.

HEROBRIAN: *(Not looking, bumps into BUBBLE)* Watch where you are going! *(Screaming angrily, tries to shock her with his powers but nothing happens. Looking at his hands)* What but- *(Whispering)* but I tried to shock her, how come?!

BUBBLE: *(Flying)* This is awesome! *(Thinking)* But how did this happen?

HEROBRIAN: *(Accidentally turning into a stranger)* Hey I can still change into other people. *(Whispering)* But I want my powers back.

*SCENE 2:* BUBBLE's house.

*(BUBBLE enters her house.)*

HEROBRIAN: *(Transforming into a girl)* Hey! I'm new around here, do you mind showing me around? *(In a friendly voice, but actually fooling her.)*

BUBBLE: Yeah! Why don't you come in?

HEROBRIAN: Sure! *(Thinking)* It just seems to be getting better and better!

BUBBLE: Do you want me to show you around my house?

HEROBRIAN: No! That's fine.

BUBBLE: *(Sitting on the couch being bored)* So what do you want to do because I'm so borrrrrred!!

HEROBRIAN: Sorry, I got to go. *(When he gets out of the house he turns back into his normal body.)*

*SCENE 3:* BUBBLE's bedroom.

*(BUBBLE stares at a door she had never seen before.)*

BUBBLE: What is that!!??

VOICE: Go in there. Go!!

BUBBLE: Who was that?!!

VOICE: Don't you know me??

BUBBLE: No!!

VOICE: I am your conscience!!

BUBBLE: Ohh! Let me go in there.

<u>SCENE 4:</u> *Inside the door, it looks like a palace with a water fountain in the middle, the water is shining.*

BUBBLE: This is beautiful.

VOICE: Well lucky for you! You have to enter this place every day. This is where you will recharge your powers. Well, since you sucked them out of Herobrian.

BUBBLE: What is that? *(Looking at a statue of the man she bumped into earlier. She hits him.)*

HEROBRIAN: *(In a low voice)* Ouch!

BUBBLE: *(Angrily)* What do you want?

HEROBRIAN: Well, now that you ask, I want my powers back— I want to *(Loud)* RULE THE WORLD! *(Softly)* For evil. *(Chuckles)*

BUBBLE: *(Loud)* I heard that!!!

HEROBRIAN: Oops!

BUBBLE: You know what?

HEROBRIAN: No!!

BUBBLE: Well, buh-bye!!! *(HEROBRIAN being destroyed!)*

*End of Play*

# Tasmania's Hypnotizing Adventure

by Mariana Resendez

Characters:
TASMANIA
FAMILY
TIGER MOM
TIGER DAD
BROTHER
SISTER
LORD VOLDEMORT
DOLLS

_SCENE 1:_ _Open land._

TASMANIA: I see grass and trees, gazelles roaming the land, I smell flowers, I taste afternoon snack, I hear wind blowing, hogs snorting. I feel grass tickling my feet. I think, "I'm free!"

_(TASMANIA and her FAMILY playing.)_

TASMANIA: This... is... so.... fun!

_(FAMILY leaves.)_

TASMANIA: Where ya goin?

FAMILY: _(Hypnotizing voice)_ We are leaving forever.

TASMANIA: _(Stammering)_ But...but...but...but...but... _(TASMANIA leaves in a scared way, follows FAMILY into open spot in the woods, sees VOLDEMORT. Whispers)_ I need a plan. _(Goes home and makes a plan.)_ You're going to help me, girls. _(TASMANIA brings out DOLLS, heads back to woods with DOLLS. Points to map.)_ You are going to be here. You are going to be here. Let's go. _(Goes back to the woods.)_

LORD VOLDEMORT: Huh? Who's there?

_(LORD VOLDEMORT goes to investigate. Drops wand.)_

TASMANIA: _(Whispers)_ Go, go, go, go.

_(DOLLS get wand, bring wand to TASMANIA.)_

TASMANIA: _(Whispers)_ Thanks. Let's go find my family!

_(Finds open spot in the woods, sees FAMILY in cage.)_

TASMANIA: Go inside and unlock the door.

_(DOLLS unlock door.)_

TASMANIA: _(Casts spell)_ Toe of dog, arm of hog, blood of worm's sting, owlet wing!!!

23

FAMILY: What just happened? What the heck? I have a giant scar down my back!

TASMANIA: Voldemort hypnotized you and I think you just have that from the spell, but I'm sure it will wear off.

BROTHER: Are the rumors true? Did we just visit Voldemort! This is so exciting!!

TASMANIA: No silly, you were hypnotized by him.

SISTER: *(Depressed voice)* Oh.

TASMANIA: You were unhypnotized with a little help from me, and my girls.

VOLDEMORT: You!!! You are such an... uhhh! I can't even talk to you because I am so mad at you!! You will all pay for this, and you are going to pay for it right... now. *(Picks her up.)*

TASMANIA: *(Higher pitched voice)* Help! ...Help!

VOLDEMORT: Ha...ha...ha. You'll never catch meee!

*(TIGER DAD roars, FAMILY chases VOLDEMORT. VOLDEMORT turns around and sticks out tongue, hits branch.)*

VOLDEMORT: *(Whispers)* Ouch.

TIGER MOM: SO what should we do with him?

*(TIGER DAD puts him in cage.)*

VOLDEMORT: Whoa, I did a pretty good job with this cage.

*(FAMILY leaves.)*

VOLDEMORT: *(Escapes, whispers)* Hee. Hee. Hee.

*To be continued...*

# The Biggest Playground

by Karla A. Cortes

Characters:
BRISA
ANDREA
CYNTHIA

_SCENE 1:_ At a park.

BRISA: I see a blue butterfly in a flower. I smell chocolate ice cream passing by. I taste fresh baked cookies. I hear bees buzzing through the flowers. I feel butterflies fluttering on my arm. I think the bird is really happy.

BRISA: Should we start building the biggest playground?!

ANDREA: Sure, I would love that!

CYNTHIA: _(She hears)_ I will destroy that playground no matter what. _(Evil laugh)_ Hahahaaa!

BRISA: Ohh no!

ANDREA: _(Whispers to BRISA)_ Let's do it somewhere else.

BRISA: _(Whispers to ANDREA)_ What a great idea Andrea!

(CYNTHIA destroys the playground material.)

CYNTHIA: Now you will never build that playground. _(Evil laugh)_ Hahaaha!

BRISA: _(Screams)_ That is not nice you evil little girl.

ANDREA: _(Screams to CYNTHIA)_ That's why you have no friends! _(Cries.)_

CYNTHIA: _(Leaves and talks evil)_ I don't care because now you're sad. Haahaaha!

BRISA: _(Talks in sad voice to ANDREA)_ Should we raise money and work?

ANDREA: _(Talks in a happy voice)_ What a great idea, and we could ask the neighbors for help.

BRISA: We can sell cookies and sell to everyone.

ANDREA: Sure, I would love that. And we can make strawberry, chocolate, and vanilla cookies!

BRISA: What are we waiting for? Let's start!

CYNTHIA: _(Talks to herself)_ They will never get away with this.

_SCENE 2:_ At BRISA's house.

ANDREA: _(Talks with BRISA)_ We just need to make sure Cynthia doesn't find out.

BRISA: I'm sure she won't find out.

CYNTHIA: *(Talks evil)* Well I just did! *(Laughs evil)* Hahahaaha.

ANDREA: *(Screams)* Leave us alone!

CYNTHIA: Or what?

BRISA: We will be friends with you.

CYNTHIA: Really?

ANDREA: Yes.

CYNTHIA: Okay.

*(They all build their playground together and get materials again.)*

*End of Play*

# *Untitled*

by Nailea Cepeda

Characters:
MELISSA
LETICIA, MELISSA's mother

*SCENE:* On the soccer field.

MELISSA: *(Screaming happily)* Perfect! We're going to start a game!

LETICIA: Melissa, would you like a gold medal?

MELISSA: *(Happily)* Of course!

LETICIA: Well if you want a gold medal you need to be in gymnastics. *(Trying to convince MELISSA to be in gymnastics.)*

MELISSA: Well maybe I don't want a gold medal because I need to be in gymnastics.

LETICIA: *(Confused)* But…

MELISSA: *(Angry)* Stop trying to convince me.

LETICIA: *(Thinks to herself)* All my plans are ruined.

MELISSA: *(Happily)* Yay!! My team and I won the game.

LETICIA: *(Looking at Melissa very angrily)* I will take her out of soccer.

MELISSA: I'm so happy.

LETICIA: Melissa, in gymnastics you can do backflips in the air. It is so easy.

MELISSA: That's so cool, maybe I think I will be in gymnastics.

LETICIA: *(Happy screaming)* Yes, finally!!

MELISSA: *(Looking at LETICIA)* What?

LETICIA: *(Serious)* Nothing!

MELISSA: Well…you must have a plan to take me out of soccer.

LETICIA: No, I don't have a plan to take you out of soccer, who said that.

MELISSA: *(Happily)* I love gymnastics, it's so cool. The good thing is that I'm in soccer and in gymnastics.

*End of Play*

# Rachel Gets Popular

by Andrea Cantu

Characters:
RACHEL, electronic device
NICKY, electronic device
NICKY'S FRIENDS, electronic devices
LILY, electronic device
JAKE, electronic device
DRAKE, electronic device

SCENE 1: *In an Apple school for iPods and iPads. RACHEL is lost in the hallways of her new school.*

RACHEL: I see all the lockers and classrooms and am wondering which one is mine and where I should go. I smell all the mechanical food in the cafeteria and the experiments of science class. I taste the sandwich in my lunch bag and think it is yummy. I hear all the electronic students talking in the cafeteria. I feel confused and also worried about not having any friends the rest of the year. I think that I am going to be fine but at the same time am not sure about that. I wish I could have some friends so I don't have to be so lonely. The lucky thing is that I have a plan. I am going to use that plan when I get to my new school.

NICKY: Friends, really? *(Laughs)* I have plenty of friends so poor you, I feel bad for you. Actually now that I think about it, I don't! *(Laughs.)*

RACHEL: *(Thinks)* Wow, I sure don't want to be her friend.

NICKY: So do you have something to say?

*(RACHEL moves her head to say no.)*

NICKY: I thought so. *(Leaves the gym and goes to change her clothes.)*

SCENE 2: *One day later.*

NICKY: *(Sees RACHEL)* Well, well, well. I guess your second day isn't going that well, right? Well that is going to continue.

*(RACHEL looks worried.)*

SCENE 3: *One hour later.*

*(NICKY throws nachos at RACHEL on purpose.)*

NICKY: Oops. *(Grins.)*

*(RACHEL sighs. NICKY laughs.)*

SCENE 4: *Two hours later.*

RACHEL: Let's see, is there a book? No!!!!!! I can't find a book of friendship.

NICKY: *(Spying on RACHEL behind a shelf)* Good thing I took all the books about friendship.

29

*SCENE 5:* *One day later.*

RACHEL: What's up girls?

NICKY'S FRIENDS: Ummm... *(They run away.)*

RACHEL: So, I can't sit with you at lunch.

*SCENE 6:* *At lunch.*

RACHEL: Let's see, is there any nice iPad to be my friend?

*(RACHEL is looking at the yearbook.)*

RACHEL: Ohhh, I found Kayla, but she loves reading so no.

*SCENE 7:* *One hour later.*

RACHEL: Let's see, nooo!!! I found no one... Wait a minute, is that Nicky? She used to wear glasses!!! Wow!!!

*SCENE 8:* *The next day.*

NICKY: So did you find any friends in the yearbook?

RACHEL: How did you know I was looking for friends in the yearbook?

NICKY: Lucky guess. *(Laughs.)*

RACHEL: *(Thinks)* Who is that new girl? Well I am going to talk to her.

LILY: Umm, hi.

RACHEL: Hi. What's your name?

LILY: Lily, I am new here.

RACHEL: Cool name, and me too. I've been here about 4 or 5 days. So do you want to sit with me at lunch?

LILY: Sure why not!

*SCENE 9:* *Two hours later.*

RACHEL: So Lily, did you see the new guy?

LILY: I did, I saw him when I was coming in.

RACHEL: He looks perfect.

*SCENE 10:* *Three hours later.*

*(RACHEL bumps into JAKE.)*

RACHEL: Oh, I'm sorry.

JAKE: I'm sorry too. Hi I'm Jake.

RACHEL: I'm Rachel. Well, bye. *(Shyly walks away.)*

*SCENE 11:* One day later.

JAKE: So hi Rachel!

RACHEL: Hi!

JAKE: So I heard there is going to be a dance.

RACHEL: Yep!!

JAKE: So do you want to go with me?

RACHEL: Sure why not!

*(RACHEL walks away with a smile. JAKE walks away with a smile.)*

*SCENE 12:* One hour later.

*(RACHEL goes screaming excited to LILY.)*

LILY: What happened?

RACHEL: The new guy asked me to the dance!

LILY: What's his name?

RACHEL: Jake.

LILY: Well, I am going with a boy named Drake.

RACHEL: Good for you. Let's go get some very cute bows.

LILY: Okay!

*SCENE 13:* The day before the dance.

NICKY: So Jake, do you have anything to say to me?

JAKE: About what?

NICKY: About the dance.

JAKE: No, I'm going with Rachel.

NICKY: What!!

*SCENE 14:* The day of the dance.

JAKE: Wow!! You look spectacular!

RACHEL: You too, and thanks. Oh, I have a surprise for you.

SCENE 15: Minutes later.

DRAKE: *(On stage)* iPads and iPhones let me present, Rachel Smith!!

*(RACHEL sings a song called "Roar" by Katy Perry.)*

SCENE 16: Minutes later.

JAKE: You were great! I have a question for you. Do you want to be my Apple friend?

RACHEL: Yes!!!

NICKY: No!!!

*(From that day on RACHEL has been more popular than NICKY.)*

*End of Play*

# *Untitled*

by Bobby Molina

Characters:
MOM
JACOB

## *SCENE 1*

MOM: *(Angry)* You're going to be grounded!

JACOB: *(Sad)* I don't want to be grounded.

MOM: Well why are you behaving bad?

JACOB: Well...

MOM: Well what?

JACOB: Well I don't like to work, that's why I behave bad.

MOM: Why don't you like the work that they give you?

JACOB: 'Cause I'm too lazy.

MOM: If you do all your work and behave good you will not be grounded.

JACOB: Fine!!

MOM: Congratulations Jacob! You are not grounded no more.

JACOB: Yes!!!

## *SCENE 2*

MOM: *(Angry)* Jacob you have been behaving bad again!

JACOB: No I didn't!

MOM: Then why did they call me that you were not paying attention.

JACOB: My friends started it.

MOM: Then why do you listen to them?

JACOB: *(Angry)* Because I'm bored, all they give me is math.

MOM: *(Angry)* Well you need to learn more math.

JACOB: *(Sadly)* Please don't ground me.

MOM: Sorry, Jacob, but you need to behave.

JACOB: I don't want to behave good.

MOM: Fine, you won't be able to play the PlayStation then.

JACOB: I don't care.

MOM: Okay you will be grounded until you are good.

JACOB: Fine I will do it.

MOM: Prove it then.

JACOB: I will.

MOM: Jacob, they called me that you were behaving good so you will not be grounded any more, but if you behave bad you will be grounded.

JACOB: I will never behave bad.

MOM: Okay.

*SCENE 3*

MOM: *(Angry)* Jacob get over here!

JACOB: What.

MOM: What were you doing in school.

JACOB: Nothing.

MOM: What do you mean nothing.

JACOB: I wasn't behaving bad.

MOM: You were behaving bad again. They called me that you weren't passing.

JACOB: Fine I was behaving bad.

MOM: *(Angry)* Why!

JACOB: Because it's hard.

MOM: It's hard because you don't pay attention.

JACOB: I was!

MOM: That's it, you're grounded.

JACOB: No!!!

MOM: Don't yell at me.

JACOB: Sorry.

MOM: I will give you one more chance.

JACOB: Deal.

MOM: Starting tomorrow.

JACOB: Okay.

MOM: Jacob, congratulations, you are not grounded! You have been passing and behaving good!

JACOB: Yeah!

*End of Play*

# The Collection Ball

by Tiare Figuroa

Characters:
BELLA, TIARE's collection soccer ball
TIARE

*SCENE: Inside.*

BELLA: *(Sad)* Why can't I be played with?

TIARE: *(Yelling)* Do you want to be kicked in your face or butt?!

BELLA: *(Scared)* Noo!

TIARE: If you say that again you won't have any air.

BELLA: I need a plan.

TIARE: Remember what I told you.

*(BELLA sprays pepper spray at TIARE.)*

BELLA: Ha! Ha!

TIARE: It burns! It burns!

*(BELLA runs outside.)*

BELLA: *(Excited)* Whoo!

*(TIARE catches BELLA and slaps her on her butt.)*

TIARE: You're not following my rules.

BELLA: *(Crying)* Ouch! Ouch!

*(BELLA makes a trap with honey.)*

BELLA: *(Laughing)* You won't escape!

*(TIARE walks into the room.)*

TIARE: Ahh! *(Honey falling over her.)*

BELLA: *(Laughing)* Haa! Haa!

TIARE: *(Angry)* Caught you!

*(BELLA puts out mouse traps.)*

BELLA: This will work.

*(TIARE walks in and gets stuck in mouse traps.)*

TIARE: Ahh!

BELLA: I have mysterious plans.

TIARE: *(Yelling)* Get back on the shelf!

BELLA: Okay.

TIARE: You can be played with.

BELLA: *(Excited)* Yeah! You hear that? It's happiness people!

*End of Play*

# *Xbox 360*

by Alexis Santiago

Characters:
ALEXIS
JHON, an Xbox

*SCENE 1*

ALEXIS: What was that noise? It sounds like Xbox tracks... Jhon! Jhon...oh brother.

JHON: *(Trying to protect himself)* Stop!

ALEXIS: Again! Why are you sneaking out again?

JHON: Because uh...I...want to turn into an Xbox One.

*(Pum!)*

ALEXIS: Ey! *(Slowly passing out)*

JHON: Ha! You thought I never will get to leave. Well I can!

ALEXIS: Uh... *(Closing his eyes)*

JHON: I finally escaped! Nothing can-

*(Pum! JHON gets hit by a car.)*

ALEXIS: *(Opening his eyes)* What happen...Aaaa! Jhon...Jhon... NOOOOOOOO!

JHON: Tick! Flushhh! *(Exploding)*

ALEXIS: I've got to save him, I made him. I can fix him. I should have thought of that when he wanted to escape.

*(Pounding with a hammer.)*

ALEXIS: Why aren't you working ey!! Calm down. Well I fixed half of him, well time to sleep. *(Snoring.)*

*(Pum!)*

ALEXIS: *(In a tired voice)* What was that?

JHON: I'm okay I just have to move with my left foot, it's hard.

ALEXIS: Let me fix the other half of you.

JHON: Okay turn me off.

ALEXIS: *(Turning him off)* I've got to fix him... *(Speaks in a really tired voice, slips really slowly falling to the ground.)*

SCENE 2: The next day.

ALEXIS: *(Yawning, breathing)* What happened last time? Where... JHON!!! *(Starts pounding with a hammer.)* I'm already done with your right eye but what about your other half? Let me turn you on.

JHON: Am I fixed?!

ALEXIS: NO.

JHON: You slept didn't you?

ALEXIS: Uh...sort of, well let me finish okay. Are you okay?

JHON: Good, but— *(Runs and jumps.)*

ALEXIS: Stop! No, stop self-destructing!

JHON: *(Exploding)* BOOOM! I smell gas, I have to get a glass of water. I taste water. I see Xbox, I smell gas, I feel painful, I hear explosions, I think I did the right thing.

*End of Play*

# *Slavvy*

by Sebastian Perez

Characters:
SLAVVY, a football
SEBASTIAN "SABY"
KID
DOCTOR

*SCENE 1: April.*

SLAVVY: I see zombies. I smell rotten skin. I taste slime. I hear "Thriller." I feel slimy. I think it's April Fools. *(Jumping up and down)* I escaped. I'm with my friends. *(Scared)* Do you hear that? *(Running)* Ahhhhhh! *(Scared)* Let me out!

SEBASTIAN: *(Screaming)* Don't do that!! *(Mad)* Bring me the disinflator. *(Evil laugh)* ha ha ha ha!

SLAVVY: Ahhhhhhhhhhhhhhhhhhhhhhhhhhhhhhhhhhhhhhhhhhhhhhh! Let me out of the chamber! *(Shouting)* Fine I don't want friends.

SABY: *(Mad)* Okay get out.

SLAVVY: But now I wanna be a spy, yup!

SABY: No.

SLAVVY: *(Grabbing a secret pen)* Mth ahhh!

*(SABY turns into a wolf.)*

SLAVVY: No! I pressed the wrong button. *(Grabs a pen)* I need to right this.

*(SLAVVY gets knocked out.)*

SLAVVY: Uhhhh.

SABY: *(Growling)* Going to make a pack. *(Breaks in a wall)* Boom!

*SCENE 2: Midnight.*

SABY: Doon doon doon doon doon. *(Confused)* What happened?

KID: You're ugly.

SABY: Uhhh.

KID: You look like poop.

SABY: Move, get out the way!

KID: You stink.

SLAVVY: Boom! Boom!

KID: *(Hearing "we uh we uh we uh")* What happened?

DOCTOR: A football trazolized you.

SLAVVY: We're on the news!

SABY: Who cares?

SLAVVY: We only have one more day to see each other.

SABY: Uhh I wish it was tomorrow.

SLAVVY: Tooooooooooooooooooooooooooo bad!

*End of Play*

# Me and X-Box: The Shield

by Sergio Rodriguez

Characters:
ME
X-BOX
KID
MOM
JOHN CENA
DANIEL BRYAN
LUKE HARPER
ERICK ROWAN
REFEREE
DOG
SWAT
FAMILY

*SCENE 1: Everywhere.*

X-BOX: I see food, I taste water, I hear people, I feel air and a storm, I think I am going to pass out, I smell oil.

ME: *(Laughing)* What up?

X-BOX: *(Angry)* What?

ME: Whoa.

X-BOX: You never play with me.

ME: Okay I'll play with you.

X-BOX: For 50 days.

ME: You're weird, no!

X-BOX: *(Crying)* Why?

ME: Because you might explode.

X-BOX: *(Scared)* Help me.

ME: Why?

X-BOX: I feel sick.

ME: *(Scared)* OMG!

X-BOX: *(Screaming)* I got you, it was a fake. I pranked you ha, ha, ha!

ME: We'll play X-Box but the score is still 60,000 to 1, peace out.

X-BOX: Do you know someone who plays?

ME: NO.

X-BOX: I am going to escape!

ME: No you're not.

X-BOX: Why?

ME: Because you can barely run 1 millimeter in like 3 hours.

X-BOX: I will create a drink called Stamin Up.

ME: With what?

X-BOX: I have no idea.

*SCENE 2:* *The street.*

X-BOX: I just found 5 things to create.

ME: You know those things are rocks.

X-BOX: Crazy kid!

ME: Why, me?

X-BOX: No not you, it was that kid that almost ran over me.

KID: Why does your X-Box speak?

ME: Because I created him.

KID: That's an ugly idea.

X-BOX: You little kid.

*(X-BOX pops KID's bicycle tire. KID goes crying to his mom.)*

MOM: What's wrong?

KID: I don't know, I just felt like I got burned from my butt.

MOM: *(Laughing)* What?

KID: *(Screaming)* I'm going to my room!

X-BOX AND ME: WOOOAH!!!

ME: Finally that kid is grounded!

X-BOX: Now can I play!

ME: Maybe.

*(X-BOX is so happy that he runs as fast as Flash.)*

X-BOX: Dude who is that?

ME: Who, that guy behind me?

X-BOX: Yeah.

ME: No way!

X-BOX: What?

ME: That is Daniel Bryan and John Cena!

X-BOX: Oh from WWE!

ME: Yeah, now let's go with them and ask them if they want to play WWE 2K14!

X-BOX: Okay.

ME: Hey guys want to go play WWE 2K14?

DANIEL BRYAN AND JOHN CENA: Okay.

ME AND X-BOX: Awesome!!!

DANIEL BRYAN: Man you're an X-pert!

ME: I know right.

JOHN CENA: Alright I need to go already.

ME: Why?

JOHN CENA: I am going to go in the ring.

X-BOX AND ME: Can we go?

JOHN CENA: Yeah.

ME AND X-BOX: Okay!

(JOHN CENA and DANIEL BRYAN against LUKE HARPER and ERICK ROWAN.)

REFEREE: Here is your winner, John Cena and Daniel Bryan!

ME: Hey dude, you still want to play until you explode?

X-BOX: No, I am better now. (Turns around and whispers "yes".)

(X-BOX tries to run away and get my BROTHER to play with him.)

ME: Traitor!!

X-BOX: What me?

ME: You wanted to play with my brother!

45

X-BOX: Okay.

*(I fall out of the window.)*

X-BOX: Where is he?

MOM: He is in the hospital and the cops won't let us in to see him.

X-BOX: You're on the hospital's roof.

MOM: Let's go see him!

X-BOX: *(Tired)* Wait for me!

DOG: Let's get him.

SWAT: You are not going in!

DOG: Why?

SWAT: Because we are going to beat him up.

FAMILY: *(Beats up SWAT team.)* You will never mess with us!

SWAT: I'm scared.

DOG: I want kibble, I'm hungry.

X-BOX: I do not want to play until I explode.

ME: I am lucky!!!

*End of Play*

# The Soccer Ball and the Minion

by Pedro Orozco

Characters:
BALL
MINION
ME

*SCENE 1*

MINION: *(Nervous)* Do you know where there is a store of bananas?

BALL: *(Happy)* Yes I know where there is a store of bananas, it's on Jackson Street.

MINION: *(Very happy)* Yes! Tomorrow I will go buy a lot of bananas.

BALL: *(Sad)* Why you need to go? I have like millions of bananas.

MINION: *(Happy)* No your bananas don't have super powers. Look, the store has a stand of the bananas that have super powers.

*(The next morning.)*

MINION: *(Very happy)* It's morning, yes? *(He puts his shoes on.)*

BALL: *(Sad)* What are you doing? Oh yeah, you are going to the banana store.

MINION: *(Nervous)* Why are you sad?

BALL: *(Crying)* Because I don't want you to go to the banana store.

*SCENE 2:* Outside of the door.

MINION: *(Very happy)* Bye, I need to go to the banana store.

BALL: *(Sad)* Don't leave please!

ME: *(Nervous)* Why are you crying?

BALL: *(Crying)* Because Minion is gone forever.

ME: *(Nervous)* Where is the Minion?

BALL: *(Sniffing)* It's on Jackson street.

ME: *(Mad)* Let's go for him.

BALL: *(Happy)* Wait I need to get my super shoes.

ME: *(Nervous)* Okay get your super shoes.

BALL: _(Happy)_ Let's go. Go so fast to get to Jackson Street!

ME: Wait, the cops will stop us.

BALL: Okay! Go little bit fast.

_SCENE 4:_ _In the banana store._

BALL: _(Slow motion)_ Don't eat the banana!

_SCENE 5:_ _In the car._

ME: You will go again to the banana store, okay?

MINION: _(Sad)_ Okay.

_End of Play_

# The Horrible Hunting

by Jesus Garcia

Characters:
JESUS
DAD
MANUEL
MAN, a zombie
ZOMBIES

SCENE 1: In the house and forest.

JESUS: (Excited) Yes yes it's my birthday!

DAD: (Excited) So that means that we are going to hunt.

JESUS: (Happy) But first we need to prepare.

DAD: Okay.

JESUS: (Running) I got the goggle glasses, rifle, and the knife.

DAD: Let's get the stuff in the car.

JESUS: Let's get in the car.

DAD: (Screaming) Okay kids we already got in the place where we're going to hunt.

JESUS: Bu... bu... bu... but tonight is so so co-old.

DAD: But we are already here, we can't go home again.

MANUEL: (Happy) I got a backpack with a thing to camp.

JESUS: (Excited) Thank you!

MANUEL: You're welcome.

DAD: That's genius...

MANUEL: Ah ah don't worry, you are my family.

SCENE 2: In the middle of the night.

(An 'Aaa' noise comes in from outside... then JESUS wakes up.)

JESUS: (Scared) What's that noise?

(JESUS wakes up MANUEL then MANUEL wakes up his DAD.)

JESUS: (Screaming) Manuel wake up!

MANUEL: *(Sleepy)* What do you want.

JESUS: You heard that?

MANUEL: What?

JESUS: That!

*(MANUEL hears the sound.)*

KIDS: *(Screaming)* Dad!!

MANUEL: Dad, Dad!

DAD: *(Waking up)* What kids?

KIDS: *(Screaming)* You hear a noise?

DAD: No I don't hear a noise.

*(The DAD hears the noise.)*

DAD: Get your guns kids, we are going to see what it is!

KIDS: Okay Dad.

DAD: Let's go out.

KIDS: Those people, they're eating something living.

DAD: Hey guy what are you doing? Come here right now.

MAN: Ha ha ah.

DAD: What did you say?

KIDS: That looks like a zombie in the movie.

DAD: You are right, that's a zombie.

KIDS: Ah Ah AH!

DAD: You kids got the real reason that they are zombies.

*(JESUS finds a plank and pulls.)*

DAD: *(Screams)* Don't pull the plank!

MANUEL: *(Nervous)* Oops too late.

DAD: Jesus, come running!

JESUS: *(Running)* Pass me the knife so I can see what it is.

DAD: No it's too late, there are more zombies.

50

JESUS: (Screaming) Pass me the rifle Manuel!

MANUEL: Okay, there it is.

JESUS: Tuff tuff, what, there's no one in here.

DAD: But I did see the zombies in the front.

(DAD hears a sound.)

DAD: What's that? Kids, come with me! Fast, fast!

KIDS: But why Dad?

DAD: Because don't you hear that sound?

KIDS: (Whispering) No, why?

(Tum tum the ZOMBIES come out behind DAD, MANUEL and JESUS.)

DAD: Ah Ah Ah the zombies bit me!

JESUS: Ch ch ch the rifle- is it okay to shoot?

MANUEL: Shoot shoot!

JESUS: Wait, it's not the time to shoot.

DAD: (Hurt) Shoot Jesus, shoot!

KIDS: Dad Dad are you ok? Dad! Dad!

MANUEL: Pick up Dad and take him to the camp.

JESUS: (Crying) Manuel you go to help Father please.

MANUEL: Okay because I am your older brother.

JESUS: And if you weren't my older brother you would be my friend.

MANUEL: Maybe, why?

DAD: Ha, kids the truck will be for you ha ha.

(The noise gets in the forest; the ZOMBIES come to the camp.)

MANUEL: Get the guns, Jesus, and pass me one and a knife.

JESUS: Okay I got the lamp.

MANUEL: Look at this box on the side of Dad. Jesus, Jesus, look in Dad's pocket to see if he has a key.

JESUS: Yes, catch the keys!

MANUEL: Jesus, take this.

JESUS: What is it?

MANUEL: A grenade.

JESUS: This is for the finale.

MANUEL: We got to go out.

*(MANUEL and JESUS go out the camp and kill the ZOMBIES. The forest appears in the news and the helicopters get MANUEL in the leg.)*

MANUEL: It's time for you to stay alive so you can be the hero.

*End of Play*

# Fight to Escape

by Hector Mata

Characters:
ME/HECTOR
MOM
DAD
SISTER
WIPY, an iPod

*SCENE 1: At home.*

FAMILY: Happy birthday to you! Happy birthday to you!

ME: It's my birthday, yeah!

MOM: We have a present, Hector.

ME: What is it Mom!? What is it Mom!?

DAD AND SISTER: It's an iPod!

MOM: We are going to Best Buy.

*(FAMILY is going to Best Buy.)*

*SCENE 2: At Best Buy.*

ME: We're here.

*(FAMILY enters Best Buy.)*

ME: Mom I want this iPod.

MOM: Okay Hector.

*(FAMILY pays and then they go home.)*

*SCENE 3: At home.*

*(HECTOR enters his room.)*

ME: I love my new iPod, his name is going to be Wipy.

WIPY: Hello I'm Wipy!

ME: What the- I heard something.

WIPY: It smells good!

ME: Do you have life?

WIPY: Yes.

ME: Okay, my name is Hector.

WIPY: My name is Wipy.

ME: Could we be friends?

WIPY: We are friends.

ME: Oh yeah!

WIPY: Where am I?

ME: In my room at my house.

WIPY: I am Superman! *(WIPY throws like Superman.)*

ME: Nooo!

*(Crack)*

ME: Wipy are you okay?

WIPY: Yes.

ME: Oh you cuts close!

WIPY: Yeah I cuts close.

ME: You are cool!

WIPY: Take me to Best Buy to be big like a person!

ME: NOOOOOOO!

WIPY: Why?

ME: Because you are going to be big.

WIPY: I'm leaving out of this house!

ME: I'm going to charge you.

WIPY: No! I hate you Hector, I hate you!

ME: You know what?

WIPY: What?

ME: Me too.

WIPY: Me too what?

ME: I hate you Wipy!

WIPY: I'm going to escape.

ME: How?

WIPY: Like this!

*(WIPY punches HECTOR.)*

ME: Ouch that hurts a lot!

WIPY: Ha ha! Bu- bu- you want me get me!

ME: Get here! *(HECTOR cracks WIPY.)* A crack!

WIPY: Hey!

ME: Let's see what you have, Wipy.

WIPY: Heee punch punch punch punch.

ME: Hee punch punch punch punch.

WIPY: I'm not going to die because I'm immortal. Hee yaa!

*(WIPY and HECTOR fight and never die.)*

ME: I'm tired.

WIPY: Me too.

ME: No Wipy, let me get my machete. *(HECTOR cuts WIPY in half.)* Yeah!

*End of Play*

# *Walking Back Home - Short Cut*

by Eduardo Acuña

Characters:
ED
JOSH
GHOST

*SCENE 1:* *Inside an abandoned house.*

ED: I think...I see a ghost.

JOSH: Where? Where is it?

ED: I think it is behind the old TV.

JOSH: I will check if it is behind the old TV.

ED: I hear a door slam *(Boom.)*

JOSH: I smell food.

ED: From where is it coming? From over there?

JOSH: Did you just touch me?

ED: No, why.

JOSH: Because I feel someone touching me.

ED: I think we're not alone.

JOSH: I think this house is haunted.

ED: You think so. I hear a little girl crying.

JOSH: I will check in that room.

ED: *(Whispering)* Wow, I think I saw a shadow.

JOSH: Well I saw the girl and then it disappeared.

ED: We have to get out of here.

JOSH: Wow!

ED: What's that?

JOSH: I don't know.

ED: You don't know what's that.

JOSH: Shhhhhhh be quiet.

ED: Wait, we have to follow the girl.

JOSH: Okay.

ED: Let's go run!

JOSH: Wait, the girl brought us to the exit.

ED: Look outside.

JOSH: It's night?

ED: Yea, we have to go home.

JOSH: Okay.

ED: All right let's go.

GHOST: Follow Ed, Josh.

*SCENE 2: At home.*

JOSH: This day was scary.

ED: Mom, we're home. Mom.

GHOST: Hoooooooooo.

JOSH: Wait a minute, is that the girl that took us to the exit?

ED: Yea.

JOSH: We have to go through the portal!

ED: Let's go.

JOSH: Jump!

ED and JOSH: Haaaaaaaaaaaaaaaaaaaaa.

*SCENE 3: Through the portal.*

ED: Where are we?

JOSH: Look!

ED: What...

 JOSH: Our mom is there.

ED: We have to stop the ghost!

GHOST: You will never stop me. Ha ha ha!

JOSH: We have to do something.

ED: Like what?

JOSH: We have to disconnect.

ED: Okay.

*End of Play*

# No Amigos

by Aaron Palma

Characters:
FRANKLIN
AARON
SERGIO
SEBASTIAN
ANGEL

FRANKLIN: I'm so bored.

AARON: I'll play with you.

FRANKLIN: No I want friends.

AARON: No, you're not going to have friends! *(Sleeping)* Zzzzzz...

*(FRANKLIN opens the window and escapes.)*

AARON: *(Wakes up)* Where's Franklin? Franklin where are you? I have your favorite food, it's chicken.

*(AARON looks for FRANKLIN around the house then he goes to FRANKLIN's room and he sees the window open.)*

AARON: Now I know where Franklin went.

FRANKLIN: *(Outside looking for friends)* Do you want to be my friend?

SERGIO: No.

AARON: I'm going to look for you Franklin.

*(AARON goes outside and gets in the car.)*

FRANKLIN: *(Asks someone)* Do you want to be my friend?

SEBASTIAN: Yes.

*(FRANKLIN and SEBASTIAN are walking together. AARON finds FRANKLIN.)*

AARON: Franklin get in the car!

FRANKLIN: No, I'm with my new friend.

AARON: What! Why are you Franklin's friend?

SEBASTIAN: Okay okay okay old man.

AARON: What did you just say to me?

SEBASTIAN: What, I didn't say anything.

AARON: *(Talking to FRANKLIN)* What did I tell you? You are no-

FRANKLIN: Yeah yeah yeah I know you said I'm not going to have a friend.

*(Doorbell rings: "ding dong ding dong!")*

AARON: I'm coming, I'm coming. *(Opens the door)* Who are you?

ANGEL: Ahahah... oh yeah, my name is Angel.

AARON: What do you want?

*(FRANKLIN gets out through the back door and climbs the fence and goes running.)*

ANGEL: Nothing bye. *(ANGEL runs.)*

AARON: That was weird. Franklin, come over here. I said Franklin, come over here! Don't tell me he just escaped again.

*(AARON runs to the car and turns it on.)*

AARON: What? It's out of gas. Shoot. I guess I have to go walking and running.

FRANKLIN: Hey, sup Sebastian.

SEBASTIAN: Sup Fran. Wait, is your name Franklin? Yeah okay, well, sup Franklin?

FRANKLIN: Ey Sebastian, come over here.

SEBASTIAN: Okay.

FRANKLIN: Let's persuade Sergio to be our friend, okay?

SEBASTIAN: Okay.

FRANKLIN: What do you have in your house?

SEBASTIAN: Well I have an Xbox and a Playstation.

FRANKLIN: So you think he will say yes? Okay let's go ask him.

SEBASTIAN: Okay.

AARON: Wwwwwait, you're not going anywhere Franklin.

FRANKLIN: But, but, I was going to persuade a guy named Sergio to come to Sebastian's house so Sergio could be our friend.

AARON: What did I tell you Sebastian? To not be Franklin's friend!

FRANKLIN: Could I go outside?

AARON: Yes but I'm going to see you through the window.

*(FRANKLIN locks the door when he goes outside.)*

60

FRANKLIN: Bye Aaron. *(Runs to SEBASTIAN)* Ah ah ah ah, sup Sebastian.

AARON: Why won't this door open?! Oh now I know why the door didn't open, it was locked and he tricked me.

*(AARON runs and looks for FRANKLIN.)*

FRANKLIN: Okay Sebastian now let's go persuade Sergio to be our friend, because maybe Aaron will find me.

SEBASTIAN: Okay let's go to Sergio's house.

FRANKLIN: *(Knocks on the door)* Knock knock knock.

SERGIO: Who is it?

FRANKLIN: It's Franklin.

SERGIO: *(Opens the door)* Oh it's you that asked me if I could be your friend.

FRANKLIN: Yeah that's me.

SEBASTIAN: Can we stop, this conversation is boring.

FRANKLIN: Okay, do you want to be our friend?

SERGIO: No.

FRANKLIN: Wwwwwwait don't close the door!

SERGIO: Why?

FRANKLIN: If you do not want to be our friend you cannot play Playstation and Xbox with us.

SERGIO: Okay okay I'll be your friend.

FRANKLIN: Let's go to Sebastian's house.

SEBASTIAN: Finally!

FRANKLIN: Yes, we made it to Sebastian's.

*(They first play the Playstation and then the Xbox.)*

SERGIO AND FRANLKIN: Sebastian, you have the cool games.

SEBASTIAN: Thanks bro.

SERGIO: I'm bored, let's go outside.

FRANKLIN AND SEBASTIAN: Yeah sure let's go.

*(AARON sees FRANKLIN from afar and runs.)*

AARON: I'm coming for you, Franklin.

FRANKLIN: Oh my god Aaron is coming, run!

*(AARON still catches FRANKLIN.)*

AARON: I'm not going to let you trick me again, and you're going to be grounded forever!

FRANKLIN: Okay, bye guys.

AARON: Now!

FRANKLIN: Okay okay.

AARON: And you, what did I tell you? To not be Franklin's friend!

SEBASTIAN: Okay.

*(AARON and FRANKLIN go walking to the house.)*

*End of Play*

# Ihascupquake's Adventure

by Valeria Portales

Characters:
IHASCUPQUAKE
OSCAR
POLICE MAN

_SCENE 1:_ _At a pet store in an adoption room for kitties._

IHASCUPQUAKE: I see kitties in cages, I smell food for dogs and cats, I taste kitten food, I hear kittens meowing for someone to adopt them. I feel the kitten's soft fur, I feel sad for the kittens. I think I should buy two cats. I should go and adopt a kitten.

_(OSCAR bumps into IHASCUPQUAKE.)_

OSCAR: _(Angrily)_ Look where you're going!

IHASCUPQUAKE: Sorry.

_(OSCAR walks away angrily.)_

OSCAR: I will get you back!

_(IHASCUPQUAKE keeps walking to the pet store.)_

OSCAR: _(Mumbles angrily)_ I should go and spy on her.

IHASCUPQUAKE: These two kittens look pretty, I will adopt them. _(She holds both kittens while going to the cashier.)_

_(OSCAR sees IHASCUPQUAKE getting out of the pet store with two cats. IHASCUPQUAKE goes to the house. OSCAR chases IHASCUPQUAKE.)_

_SCENE 2:_ IHASCUPQUAKE's house.

IHASCUPQUAKE: Finally, we're here! _(Gets both kittens and gets inside the house.)_

_(OSCAR hides behind a bush.)_

IHASCUPQUAKE: OH, I need to buy some milk, stay here.

_(OSCAR goes inside, sneaking. IHASCUPQUAKE sees OSCAR getting out of her house with her kittens. OSCAR takes the two kittens to a little house by the river.)_

_SCENE 3:_ OSCAR's house.

IHASCUPQUAKE: What is he doing with my cats?

OSCAR: Now Ihascupquake will never find you.

_(IHASCUPQUAKE sneaks into OSCAR's house. OSCAR gets both kittens and tries to throw the kittens in the river.)_

IHASCUPQUAKE: Not so fast! *(Runs as fast as she can and pushes OSCAR and gets both kittens.)*

OSCAR: Hey! *(Stands up.)*

*(IHASCUPQUAKE grabs OSCAR's hands and puts him in her car.)*

OSCAR: Hey, where are you taking me?!

IHASCUPQUAKE: To the police.

*SCENE 4:* At the police station.

*(BOTH get out of the car.)*

IHASCUPQUAKE: This guy tried to steal my cats.

POLICE MAN: Okay, he will stay in the woods for 50 days.

OSCAR: NOOO!

*End of Play*

# Cookie vs. Melissa

by Jocelyn Bernal

Characters:
COOKIE
MELISSA

_SCENE 1_: An elementary school, in the hallway outside the classroom.

COOKIE: I see kids, classrooms, teachers, kids' works. I smell cafeteria lunch, juice. I taste juice, pizza, ice cream. I hear kids laughing, teachers talking. I feel the kids are noisy. I think I want to get one more ice cream.

_SCENE 2_: Later

COOKIE: Melissa, you know that I'm going to take your powers.

MELISSA: _(Loud voice)_ Why?

COOKIE: Because you are doing things that you don't need to do.

MELISSA: Okay I'm not going to do those things any more.

COOKIE: Okay, better not Melissa, because I'm going to tell your parents if you do that stuff.

MELISSA: Okay.

COOKIE: If you do it again I'm not going to be your friend.

MELISSA: Who cares, I'm not your friend because you're mean to me.

_SCENE 3:_ At COOKIE's house.

(COOKIE goes to her house and put the powers on the table. Then MELISSA comes and steals her powers.)

MELISSA: Victory is mine!

COOKIE: _(Loud voice)_ Why?

MELISSA: Because you're mean and I stole from you Cookie, now I'm going to hurt people!

COOKIE: NOOO! I'm going to do it to you Melissa.

_End of Play_

# The Teddy Bear

by Mercy Romero

Characters:
SAMY, AMY's teddy bear
AMY

SAMY: I have magic and I want to have friends.

AMY: *(Screaming)* Do not use magic.

SAMY: *(Whispers)* I don't care.

AMY: Come here Samy!

SAMY: *(Sad)* Oooh not to the room.

AMY: *(Screaming)* Hurry up!

SAMY: I don't like to come to the room.

AMY: Why don't you like to come?

SAMY: Because you don't let me go to the store with you and you don't let me have friends.

AMY: I don't let you have friends because you are gonna go with other friends all day and you are not gonna come home until the night.

SAMY: I don't want to have friends to do that. I want to have my friends come and play with me.

AMY: Okay, we are gonna go to the store but you can have friends, and we are going to go to the Build-A-Bear store because you are gonna know friends.

SAMY: Yessss. *(Whispers)* Okay go into the car. But my mom cannot see you.

*(They get to the store.)*

SAMY: Ooooo!

AMY: First we are gonna go to a store to buy you clothes.

SAMY: Can I choose the clothes?

AMY: Yes, you can choose.

SAMY: I want this, that, this one looks pretty, that, this.

AMY: *(Screaming)* Stop, that's too many clothes! For that reason I'm not gonna let you have friends.

*End of Play*

# The Tablet

by Jovanna Ramirez

Characters:
ANA
ROSA

*SCENE 1: One day ANA is playing with ROSA's tablet.*

ANA: Hello Rosa.

ROSA: Hello Ana. Ana, can I borrow the tablet?

ANA: No! *(They are fighting over the tablet.)*

ROSA: Give me the tablet!

ANA: Give me the tablet!

ROSA: No give me the tablet! *(ROSA takes away the tablet.)*

*(ROSA goes to ANA's house. ANA is crying. In the night ANA goes to ROSA's house. ANA is checking where the tablet is.)*

ROSA: What was that noise?

*(ANA transforms invisible and escapes.)*

*SCENE 2: The next day.*

*(ANA goes to ROSA's house.)*

ANA: Rosa, can we be friends?

ROSA: *(Thinking)* I don't know, Ana.

ANA: Okay Rosa.

*(In the night ANA goes to ROSA's house. ANA transforms invisible. She gets the tablet. The next day ROSA looks for the tablet.)*

ROSA: Where is the tablet, where did I put it?

*(ROSA goes to ANA's house.)*

ROSA: What? Did you have the tablet, Ana, and how did you get it?

ANA: I entered your house in the night.

ROSA: Can we be friends?

ANA: Yes.

ROSA: Okay.

ANA: Friends forever.

ROSA: Friends forever, okay.

*End of Play*

# The Adventures of Xbox 360 and his Amazing Friend Controller

by Joaquin Soto

Characters:
XBOX 360
CONTROLLER
ROBOCOP
STRANGERS

*SCENE 1:* Area 51.-1.

XBOX 360: I see danger signs (a dangerous area), I smell toxic stuff, I taste venom, I hear bombs, I feel somebody is watching me, I think it's not dangerous. I wish I was an Xbox One because I am not popular. The good thing is that I have a plan and with my controller friend the plan will work great. Hey controller, haven't you imagined being an Xbox One?

CONTROLLER: Sometimes.

XBOX 360: Well I got a plan. *(He didn't even have a plan and is trying to think of a plan while taking a long time.)*

CONTROLLER: Well what is it?

XBOX 360: *(Says it very fast)* First we have to go on a plane to go to area 51.-1 to get the machines.

CONTROLLER: What about the cop?

XBOX 360: Well, I didn't think of that.

CONTROLLER: Well I have powers.

XBOX 360: So what are we waiting for? Let's do the job.

*SCENE 2:*

XBOX 360: *(Very happy)* I can't believe we are doing a dangerous job.

CONTROLLER: *(Scared)* I do believe it!

*(Moments later.)*

XBOX 360: Yes, we're here!

CONTROLLER: Oh no.

XBOX 360: Oh yes.

*(ROBOCOP comes in madly.)*

71

ROBOCOP: Get out of here, this is super secret!

XBOX 360: *(Asking himself)* How is it super secret if it's in the middle of a big city?

ROBOCOP: *(Says madly and embarrassed)* Oh, uh........stand back.

XBOX 360: Okay, okay we will get out of here.

CONTROLLER: We can't leave!!!!

ROBOCOP: *(Backstage)* I am going to count to three... One, *(skips number two)* three! *(Shooting electrical bullets and making an evil laugh)* Ha, ha, ha!

XBOX 360: *(Really scared and giving a really girly scream)* Aaaaaahhhhh!

*SCENE 3:*

XBOX 360: *(Screaming out loud)* Use your powers, controller!!!!!!!!

CONTROLLER: Okay, you don't have to scream!!!!

*(CONTROLLER uses his powers and only has 1%.)*

CONTROLLER: Oh no.

XBOX 360: What?

CONTROLLER: We're doomed.

*(Moments later.)*

CONTROLLER: *(Looking for batteries)* I got some batteries.

XBOX 360: Well do it! *(Blows ROBOCOP away.)*

*(XBOX 360 and CONTROLLER go to the lab to be an Xbox One. They leave and ROBOCOP comes.)*

ROBOCOP: I will get revenge in 40 years!

*(STRANGERS look at him and ask themselves what he is doing.)*

*To be continued...*

# Who Is Going to Be the Main Character?

by Valeria Pech

Characters:
BAMBOO
SAM

_SCENE 1:_ A film set.

BAMBOO: I see people with big cameras. I am so nervous. I smell food in the room and it makes me hungry. I taste the sweat in my mouth. I hear music and people talking to other people. I feel very nervous. I think I could make the act if I am not nervous. Because I could sing and dance with people.

SAM: _(Screaming)_ Bamboo, let me be the main character!

BAMBOO: No! You will not because I told you about this.

SAM: _(Angry)_ An-

BAMBOO: _(Crying)_ Quiet! I'm gonna be the main character! Now go because you are not my friend anymore.

SAM: Don't you dare talk to me Bamboo!

BAMBOO: I could talk to you like that because I don't know you. _(BAMBOO copies him.)_

SAM: This is what you get! _(Pushes him in the closet and locks it with his powers.)_ Sorry. _(Sighs.)_

BAMBOO: I will give you something.

SAM: What is it?

_SCENE 2:_ I will give you something.

BAMBOO: Do you believe in me?

SAM: I don't know.

BAMBOO: C'mon.

SAM: Fine, what will you give me?

BAMBOO: I don't know.

SAM: Do you know what an iPhone is?

_(BAMBOO is confused.)_

SAM: Just give me something.

BAMBOO: Okay. I will give you a dollar.

SAM: Are you serious, really, no!

(BAMBOO sighs.)

BAMBOO: I will clean your room, please.

SAM: You said you were not my friend.

BAMBOO: Fine, we will change every time.

SAM: Okay. *(Lets him free.)*

*SCENE 3:* Survive.

SAM: Oh, man! I am so happy.

BAMBOO: Me first, okay.

SAM: Okay. Bamboo.

BAMBOO: What.

SAM: Bye. *(Pushes him with his powers.)*

BAMBOO: Where am I?

SAM: Let me call him.

BAMBOO: Hello.

SAM: You are in a jungle.

BAMBOO: Noooooo!

SAM: You will stay there forever. Hahaha.

BAMBOO: Please don't leave m- Hello? I need food. Good thing I know how to catch a fish. Oh I have my food, okay let's eat.

*(Two years later. Noise effect: thunthunthun!)*

BAMBOO: Now that I did this machine I will go back.

*SCENE 4:* Going home.

BAMBOO: Okay, let me just turn it on. Let's go. I'm going to talk to Sam.

*(Takes machine back to SAM's house.)*

BAMBOO: Let me just dress up as someone.

SAM: Where is my room?

BAMBOO: It's a surprise, close your eyes.

SAM: Okay.

BAMBOO: Go straight, now bye Sam.

SAM: Wait what no.

BAMBOO: Now who is in the jungle?

SAM: Good, I am at my house. Wait not again. No!

BAMBOO: He learned his lesson. I'm sorry Sam.

SAM: Friends.

BAMBOO: Friends.

BAMBOO AND SAM: Friends forever!

*End of Play*

# *Untitled*

by Angel Mendoza

Characters:
ANGEL
STEVE, a soccer ball
BUBBLE GUM, a basketball
OTHER BALLS
CAR

*SCENE 1*: *At ANGEL's home, in the living room.*

ANGEL: Let's go outside, Steve!

STEVE: No! I don't want to get dirty.

ANGEL: I want to play soccer with my friends and you need to come with me to play.

STEVE: I don't want to go play and you can't force me to play.

ANGEL: Yes I can.

STEVE: No you can't.

ANGEL: Yes I can!

STEVE: If you can, come on.

ANGEL: If you don't come I won't let you play inside.

STEVE: I don't care.

ANGEL: I'm gonna get you. Here, I got you now. Let's go outside.

STEVE: Ouch! Ouch! Ouch! If you don't let me go I'm gonna tickle you... 123 tickle tickle!

ANGEL: Ha! Ha! Ha! Ha! Stop stop stop!!! *(ANGEL is laughing.)*

STEVE: Okay, don't be mad.

ANGEL: Now go to the basement, now!

STEVE: Okay.

*(Sad "squak squak squak" sound effect. Basement door opens. Puff! Basement door closes.)*

*SCENE 2*: *In ANGEL's basement.*

STEVE: Where's the light? I don't see nothing.

BUBBLE GUM: Hey!

77

STEVE: Who is it? Who is it?

BUBBLE GUM: Pom pom pom, *(Ball bouncing)* thik thuk. *(Lights on)*

STEVE: *(Yelling)* Ha! Ha! Ha! Go away from me!

BUBBLE GUM: I won't hurt you, I'm Bubble Gum the basketball.

STEVE: I'm trying to 'scape from Angel Mendoza.

BUBBLE GUM: Me too. A long time ago Angel Mendoza forced me to go outside every day when I was tired too.

STEVE: We need a plan to get out of this problem. Okay, first we need to make a door on the roof and get a flashlight for if we get lost. Now we need to where we are going.

BUBBLE GUM: We can go to a little place where Angel Mendoza made a house.

STEVE: I know a place we can go so Angel Mendoza cannot find us. The place is in his old house, he never goes to his old house.

BUBBLE GUM: This night we are gonna get out of this old basement- let's go.

STEVE: Let's do a hole on the roof. Pom! Pom! Uugh poom! Bubble Gum, let's go. I already made the hole on the roof.

BUBBLE GUM: No way, it's night, let's get our flashlights.

*(Flashlights turning on.)*

STEVE: First let's go to the little place where Angel made the house.

SCENE 3: Outside of ANGEL's house.

BUBBLE GUM: Let's go running so we can get there fast.

STEVE: Ugh, I'm tired Bubble Gum.

BUBBLE GUM: We're here, let's get in the house. Steve, look, here's stuff.

STEVE: Let's take a break.

BUBBLE GUM: *(Asleep)* Me me me.

STEVE: Bubble Gum are you asleep?

CAR: Truk truk truk.

STEVE: Bubble Gum, Angel is here let's get out of fast!

BUBBLE GUM: What what what?

STEVE: Angel is here!

BUBBLE GUM: Let's run.

ANGEL: Steve, are you here?

STEVE: Ugh ugh ugh.

BUBBLE GUM: Ugh ugh ugh.

STEVE: Where are we?

BUBBLE GUM: I don't know, I think we are in the woods. Now where's Angel's old house?

STEVE: I don't know, I think we are lost.

BUBBLE GUM: Let's keep walking.

STEVE: I think we're here.

BUBBLE GUM: Oh my god it's so big and old but I don't care.

STEVE: This is our destiny.

BUBBLE GUM: Yes! We lost Angel! Hooray! He has stinky socks!

(Sound: squeaking of the door.)

SCENE 4: In ANGEL's old house.

STEVE: Let's go to Angel's room, there's some stuff.

BUBBLE GUM: Steve! Come on up.

STEVE: I'm going. What?

BUBBLE GUM: Look at this!

STEVE: What is that?

BUBBLE GUM: I don't know but it looks cool.

STEVE: Somebody came in. Ha! Ha! Who are you?

OTHER BALLS: We are Angel's balls, he left us in this old house. They are my friends.

STEVE: Hi, me and him are Angel's balls too.

OTHER BALLS: Oh.

STEVE: Do you want to be our friends?

OTHER BALLS: Oh yeah for sure.

STEVE: Okay great.

End of Play

# *Untitled*

by Julissa Zepeda

Characters:
BON-BON
JULISSA

BON-BON: Hi Julissa.

JULISSA: Hi Bon-Bon.

BON-BON: Your mom is doing tacos and I want to eat them.

JULISSA: Ha, ha ha I just ate tacos right nawww!

BON-BON: I need to go to the restroom.

JULISSA: No! You are just wobbling your bottom.

BON-BON: *(Starts crying)* Aaa Julissa am I going to get real friends?

*(JULISSA is so sad.)*

BON-BON: I want to go to Julissa's house *(Starts crying)* and smell tacos. Aaaaa!

JULISSA: I am a bad person but Bon-Bon is too.

*(BON-BON comes back to JULISSA's home.)*

JULISSA: I don't want you.

*(BON-BON goes to the street.)*

JULISSA: Stop I want you. Come and I will read you a story.

*(And they all lived happily ever after now. JULISSA and BON-BON were happy.)*

*End of Play*

# The Rich Cat

by Shantal Cazarez

Characters:
ROCKY, a cat
TITO, a dog
FRENCH CATS


_SCENE:_ _In a rich house._

ROCKY: I see a dog playing on a tablet. I smell food baking. I taste milk. I hear DogTube. I feel nice people doing what I want. I think I should order some dog meal.

_(To TITO.)_

ROCKY: Finally we are front to front, may I please have some of your money so I could be rich like you.

TITO: _(Thinks and sighs)_ I don't know because you have been mean to me.

ROCKY: Okay I'm being serious, _(Frowns and is mad)_ if you don't do what I tell you to do you are going to suffer the consequences.

TITO: Okay! I have to get out of here.

ROCKY: Now I'm rich and I have a tablet and a big house for my own.

_(Now the cat disappears and everybody from the pet store misses him.)_

TITO: These are some examples of how you have been mean to me: you have stolen from me, you ignored me when I needed you. I left to France with my family and I became rich again.

FRENCH CATS: How did you become famous?

TITO: Just singing with my band. _(Leaves in a limousine.)_

_(One day the cat came back and met the dog again. The dog became poor again and the cat left to France and people say that the cat became rich again.)_

_End of Play_

# The Charger

by Daphne Camacho

Characters:
TUTU
SHERRY

TUTU: I wish I could have a friend to play with. Because I think I am going to stay alone forever. I wish for someone to be my best friend forever. I am so happy to see the store.

SHERRY: You are still a little tablet to talk with me.

TUTU: Why are you so mean?

SHERRY: Because I have already come to this store for three weeks.

TUTU: I want to talk to you because I am new and I don't have any friends.

SHERRY: You will not have any friends in this store.

TUTU: You are so mean! What's wrong with—

SHERRY: *(Mad)* STOP!!!

TUTU: What.

SHERRY: I am really bad. Do you want your battery to finish?

TUTU: NO!

SHERRY: Okay, they will take us out of this box to another one.

TUTU: Okay.

SHERRY: Bye.

TUTU: This is a long and a big store.

SHERRY: Ay!! I am next to Tutu.

TUTU: Hey Sherry, we are next to each other.

*Middle.*

SHERRY: *(Scared)* Oh no.

TUTU: What happened to you?

SHERRY: I do not have more battery, only 5%.

TUTU: Oh no!

SHERRY: Can you lend me your charger?

TUTU: I have another type of charger. I will tell someone to lend me the same charger as yours.

SHERRY: I stay alone again.

TUTU: *(Thinking)* She has no battery, that's bad. How am I going to go to the place of chargers?

SHERRY: *(Alone in a box)* I feel bad with not much battery. *(Scared)*

TUTU: Oh here comes a man. *(TUTU gets on a box.)*

SHERRY: *(Crying)* I don't like to sleep so much.

TUTU: *(Happy)* Yes, I am here at the chargers place.

SHERRY: *(Mad)* Why is he taking a lot of time? I am going to sleep for so, so, so, so much time.

TUTU: Oh no! I don't know what type of charger that Sherry used.

SHERRY: No!!! Why does this happen to me?

TUTU: What am I going to do if I don't know what type of charger she uses?

SHERRY: Okay, ready to go to sleep for so much time.

TUTU: Oh there's a phone like Sherry and there is a charger.

SHERRY: I will sleep for a little time so my battery won't finish.

TUTU: *(Screaming)* Sherry, Sherry!!!!!!! I have your charger.

SHERRY: *(Gets up)* Oh you have one like mine.

TUTU: Put it on.

SHERRY: The charger doesn't work.

TUTU: Don't worry, I will go for help.

Sherry: Hurry Tutu hurry!

TUTU: I need paper and a pencil.

Sherry: On the table there's paper and a pencil, use them.

TUTU: I will write, "Phone number 5 needs a charger."

SHERRY: Jump, Tutu, there's a man coming.

TUTU: *(Jumps to the floor)* Yes, the man got the paper.

SHERRY: *(So happy)* Here comes a man with a charger!

TUTU: You see!!! My idea was good, the man gave you a charger.

*(Later.)*

SHERRY: Thanks Tutu, know you are my best friend.

TUTU: *(Jumping, so happy)* You too!!!

*End of Play*

# The Happiest Girl

by Julissa Solis

Characters:
MONSERRAT
TAYLOR
ALEJANDRO

*ACT 1, SCENE 1:* *In iPad City.*

MONSERRAT: I see the Statue of Liberty. I smell the salty sea. I taste the sweetness of the chocolate bars. I hear the musicians playing along. I feel proud of being here but lonely. I think this place is awesome. *(Talking to the audience)* I wish that I wouldn't live lonely and alone. I would like to have a boyfriend that loves me. Also I would like a friend.

*ACT 1, SCENE 2:* *In MONSERRAT's house.*

*(MONSERRAT meets TAYLOR.)*

MONSERRAT: Oh hello Taylor. It's nice to meet you.

TAYLOR: *(Mysterious voice)* I have a secret, Monserrat.

MONSERRAT: *(Coughing)* What is it, Taylor?

TAYLOR: I'll tell you if you promise me something, Monserrat.

MONSERRAT: What's the promise? Oh, and tell me the secret first, Taylor.

TAYLOR: Okay Monserrat, I'll tell you. The secret is that I like Alejandro!!!!

MONSERRAT: *(In a mad mood and screaming)* No!!!!!!!!!!!!!  Alejandro is mine!

TAYLOR: Okay let's go and ask who Alejandro really likes.

*ACT 2, SCENE 1:*

ALEJANDRO: *(In a sweet way)* Hello Monserrat and Taylor.

TAYLOR: We want you to say who you really like.

ALEJANDRO: That's a secret of mine.

TAYLOR: *(In a sad way)* Why?

*(ALEJANDRO leaves the room and goes outside.)*

TAYLOR: I think he won't tell us.

MONSERRAT: Fine, but he is still mine.

TAYLOR: Noo!

MONSERRAT: YES!

TAYLOR: No!

87

*(MONSERRAT goes to ask ALEJANDRO something.)*

MONSERRAT: Please Alejandro, tell me who you like, I'll do whatever so you can tell me.

ALEJANDRO: I'll think about it.

*ACT 3, SCENE 1:* At *MONSERRAT's house.*

*(ALEJANDRO knocks at MONSERRAT's house)*

MONSERRAT: Yes, who is it?

ALEJANDRO: It's me, Alejandro.

MONSERRAT: What do you want Alejandro?

ALEJANDRO: Do you want to hang out?

MONSERRAT: Yeah.

ALEJANDRO: Okay, I'll see you tomorrow at 6:30pm.

MONSERRAT: I'll see you at my house.

ALEJANDRO: Bye Monserrat *(Gives MONSERRAT a kiss on the cheek.)*

*(The next afternoon at 6:30.)*

MONSERRAT: Hi Alejandro. How are you?

ALEJANDRO: Fine, how are you?

MONSERRAT: Fine too.

ALEJANDRO: Let's watch a movie.

MONSERRAT: Did you think about it?

ALEJANDRO: *(Looking up and grabbing her chin)* Ummm yeah I did.

MONSERRAT: So what?

ALEJANDRO: I will not tell you anyway.

MONSERRAT: Please Alejandro, *(Leaning on the floor)* tell me, *(Crying)* I will do anything for you. I will clean your house.

ALEJANDRO: Umm okay, I will tell you.

MONSERRAT: Who is it? Why don't you tell us two?

ALEJANDRO: Okay, the one I like is Monserrat.

TAYLOR: Nooooooooooo!

*End of Play*

# *Untitled*

by Iceth Romero

Characters:
JULISSA
KITTEN

*SCENE 1:* At the beach.

JULISSA: I smell my kitten. I see my kitten play with his friend on the beach. I taste the water. I hear people talking. I feel happy. I think this is cool.

KITTEN: That is my food, Julissa.

JULISSA: But I want to eat your food.

KITTEN: Noooo!

JULISSA: Can I drink from your milk?

KITTEN: Yes!

JULISSA: Thank you!

KITTEN: But not my food.

JULISSA: But can I eat a little bit.

KITTEN: Nooooo Julissa!

JULISSA: Okay.

KITTEN: Julissa do you want to be friends again?

JULISSA: Yes, I do want you to be my friend.

KITTEN: You can be my best friend!

JULISSA: Now can I eat your food?

KITTEN: Yes, you can eat my food.

JULISSA: Yes, I'm so hungry.

KITTEN: Yes sure Julissa.

JULISSA: Thank you Kitten!

KITTEN: You're welcome Julissa.

JULISSA: I'm going to go to my house, Kitten.

KITTEN: Ok Julissa.

JULISSA: Bye.

KITTEN: Bye Julissa.

*SCENE 2:*

JULISSA: I'm going to go to my house.

KITTEN: I'm going to drink my milk!

JULISSA: Hi Kitten.

KITTEN: Hi Julissa.

JULISSA: Could I play with you?

KITTEN: I'm going to my bed.

JULISSA: Why?

KITTEN: I'm so sleepy.

JULISSA: Okay.

KITTEN: Bye.

JULISSA: Bye Kitten.

KITTEN: Do you want to play with me?

JULISSA: Yes I want to play with you.

KITTEN: I have a new toy.

JULISSA: Can I see the toy?

KITTEN: Yes but you can't play with the toy.

JULISSA: Why not?

KITTEN: Do you want to play with my toy?

JULISSA: What?

KITTEN: You have to give me 10 dollars.

JULISSA: What, you want 10 dollars?

KITTEN: Yes 10 dollars.

JULISSA: To play with your toy?

KITTEN: And also if you want my toy.

JULISSA: Yes I want your toy, Kitten.

KITTEN: 50 dollars.

SCENE 3:

KITTEN: If you win the race you get the toy.

JULISSA: Yes I am going to win.

KITTEN: You are not going to give me 1 dollar.

JULISSA: Okay.

KITTEN: If you win in the race.

JULISSA: What?

KITTEN: You are not going to give me 20 dollars.

JULISSA: Okay you said it, Kitten.

KITTEN: Are you ready, start.

(JULISSA is in the middle. KITTEN is almost done.)

JULISSA: Noo you won!

KITTEN: Give me 10 dollars and 50 dollars.

JULISSA: Okay.

KITTEN: Too bad too sad Julissa.

JULISSA: What?

KITTEN: You loser.

JULISSA: But I was about to reach the end.

KITTEN: You are not getting my toy.

JULISSA: I am going to give you 1 dollar and 10 dollars.

KITTEN: What? Nooo!

JULISSA: Now I win. Bye, I am going to give you the money.

KITTEN: Okay bye.

JULISSA: I'll see you tomorrow.

End of Play

# Executive Director's Note

by Brigitte Pribnow Moore, YPT Executive Director

Dear Friends,

It is my great honor to join you in celebrating the incredible young people of Graciela Garcia Elementary School. We are inspired by the hard work and joyful energy of Garcia's 2013-14 fourth graders, and we are proud to share their beautiful plays in this book.

At YPT, we dream of a world where every student knows the power of her own voice. When Catherine DiSanza approached me with the idea to launch our *In-School Playwriting Program* at Garcia Elementary School, I knew in my gut that we had to yes. We had never provided our flagship program outside of the DC metro area before. In fact, we had never taught students outside of an urban setting. We had no idea how Garcia's students would react to outsiders coming into their school and urging them to tell their stories. But we knew we couldn't pass up the opportunity to share what we've learned in Washington, DC over the past twenty years with the young people of the Rio Grande Valley – students who have such rich voices and ideas to share.

When we visited Garcia for the first time in February of 2014, I knew we'd picked the right school for this pilot program. At Garcia, every wall is overflowing with student work, every child walks through the halls smiling and every teacher sparkles with passion for her students and her curriculum. We were warmly welcomed by Garcia's students, faculty, staff and the Pharr-San Juan-Alamo community at large. I can't tell you how grateful we are that the Garcia family took a chance on this program.

At YPT, we are committed to having a tangible impact on the students we serve—not just on their creativity and self-expression, but on their mastery of the English language and their ability to articulate their thoughts clearly. This aspect of our program was especially important at Garcia, where every student is bilingual and 83% of students are considered to be of Limited English Proficiency. We were overjoyed to learn that our fourth graders **improved their writing by 7 points and their reading by 11 points** over the 2012-13 STAAR exams. We also received reports of many fourth graders speaking English more confidently and generally "coming out of their shells" during the time we spent with them. These students should be proud beyond measure of their accomplishments, as we are proud to have played even a small role in their journey.

Fortunately, that journey continues, for both YPT and Garcia. Thanks to additional support from the school and the PSJA Independent School District, we are able to resume our *In-School Playwriting Program* at Garcia for the 2014-15 school year—and we are expanding into a new grade level! We are delighted that Catherine is not only teaching this year's fourth graders, but also has the chance to reunite with the now-fifth graders for another semester of exploring the joy and power of playwriting.

Thank you to each and every student, teacher and administrator at Garcia who embraced our program so openly, and particularly to Principal Yolanda Castillo, an inspiring leader whom we greatly admire. We hope to continue our *In-School Playwriting Program* at Garcia for years to come, and to expand to other schools in the region. Please help us achieve that dream by sharing this book with your friends and family. Your support makes a world of difference in the lives of our students – in DC and in the Rio Grande Valley.

Thank you, from the bottom of my heart, for believing in the power of arts education to change lives, and in the unstoppable potential of our young people.

Warmly,

Brigitte Pribnow Moore, Executive Director, Young Playwrights' Theater

# About YPT

Young Playwrights' Theater (YPT) is the only professional theater in Washington, DC dedicated entirely to arts education. Our mission is to inspire young people to realize the power of their own voices. By teaching students to express themselves through the art of playwriting, YPT develops students' language skills, and empowers them with the creativity, confidence and critical thinking skills they need to succeed in school and beyond. YPT honors its students by involving them in a high-quality artistic process where they feel simultaneously respected and challenged and by engaging professional theater artists in producing student plays for the community.

### YPT's Guiding Principles and Beliefs

**Each student has a story worth telling.** We believe the stories that our students have to tell are valuable and provide communities with a powerful perspective about the youth experience. The YPT process invites students to share their ideas, dreams and beliefs through the playwright's craft.

**The arts are critical to excellence in education**. We believe that theater and the art of playwriting are powerful tools in developing creativity and self-expression and in fostering learning across disciplines.

**The process is more important than the product.** We involve students in an ongoing creative process that enhances their learning and literacy while providing them with appropriate building blocks to construct a play. While we strive for artistic excellence, we believe the effect of the YPT process is ultimately more important than the work produced.

**We strive for high standards from all who participate in our programs.** The YPT process honors and respects the value of the work of its professional artists, students and partners. YPT expects the same self-discipline and respect from students as it does from the professionals involved in the process.

**We meet students where they are.** By reaching out to students through organized in-school, after-school and summer programs at neighborhood schools and community centers, YPT provides students of diverse backgrounds with a supportive environment where they can exchange ideas and express themselves freely.

Young Playwrights' Theater
Brigitte Pribnow Moore, Executive Director
Karen Zacarías, Founding Artistic Director

2437 15th Street NW
Washington, DC 20009
(202) 387-9173
www.yptdc.org

www.ingramcontent.com/pod-product-compliance
Lightning Source LLC
Chambersburg PA
CBHW052341100426

42736CB00046B/3323